Kokila
An imprint of Penguin Random House LLC, New York

Visit us online at penguinrandomhouse.com

Library of Congress Cataloging-in-Publication Data is available.

Printed in China
ISBN 9780525555094

1 3 5 7 9 10 8 6 4 2

Design by Jasmin Rubero
Text set in Breughel Com

The art for this book was created digitally using hand drawings and collage pieces.

FAUJA SINGH KEEPS GOING

THE TRUE STORY OF THE OLDEST PERSON TO EVER RUN A MARATHON

by **SIMRAN JEET SINGH**

illustrated by **BALJINDER KAUR**

Kokila

For Jiya Sundari Kaur and Azaadi Amro Kaur

—S. J. S.

For everyone who has been my faith when I have been my doubt.

Thank you for keeping me going.

—B. K.

FOREWORD

All my life, people set limitations on me. They said I would never walk. Then they said I would never farm. They certainly never thought I would set records with my running. No matter what people said, I always believed in myself. I knew my body better than anyone else. I knew what I was capable of. I kept trying. I never gave up. And I always held on to hope.

I wish the people from my birthplace of Punjab could see me now. The boy they teased for not being able to walk became the oldest person to ever run a marathon. I was the first 100-year-old to ever run 26.2 miles.

Doctors couldn't figure out why I had trouble walking as a child, nor could they figure out why I was able to begin walking and, eventually, running. I think of it as a reminder that all of our bodies are different—and so are our experiences with disabilities.

I'm now 108 years old, which means I'm probably more than 100 years older than you. Can you believe that?

My secret to a long and healthy life has been taking care of my mind, body, and soul. Every day, I challenge myself to think, exercise, eat healthy, and pray. I have really enjoyed my long life and hope you have a long and happy life too. I'd love for you to take care of yourself, try your hardest, and always choose yes when you meet a challenge. And who knows? Maybe one day you can break my record for the oldest person to ever run a marathon. Nothing would make me happier!

FAUJA SINGH

It was a sweltering summer.

Little Fauja Singh sat under the shade of a banyan tree in his village in Punjab, eating mangoes and watching the other children play.

Fauja was smart and funny. He and his friends liked to play cards and marbles while sitting in a circle and telling jokes.

But Fauja longed to join them when they ran and jumped.

He longed to play hopscotch, to rescue a runaway cricket ball, or to run with a kite flying high across the sky.

He wished he felt as strong as his name, which meant "warrior lion"!
When he was very little, his parents thought that he might never walk.
Month after month and year after year went by, but Fauja did not take a single step.
Aunts and uncles, grandmas and grandpas shook their heads gravely and said:
"It's too hard. He's too weak."

But Fauja did not listen and Fauja did not stop.
Instead, every morning he would listen to his mother,
who said: "You know yourself, Fauja, and you know what
you're capable of. Today is a chance to do your best."

Fauja practiced walking outside his family's hut each day, staying in the mud to soften every fall.

He practiced and prayed for months. He could feel himself getting stronger, inside and out.

Then, a few days after Fauja's fifth birthday, a wonderful thing happened.

He took one step…
And another…

Then another,
and another,
and another!

Fauja Singh was finally walking!

Fauja's parents were proud that their son understood what he was capable of and that he worked hard to achieve his goals. They were thrilled Fauja could walk because they knew it would make his life easier. His parents were so happy, they shared prayers of thanks and distributed parshad to the entire village.

Once Fauja began to walk, his legs needed strengthening.

He practiced walking around the banyan tree every day. Some bullies thought his legs looked like sticks, and they teased Fauja by calling him "danda."

But Fauja did not listen and Fauja did not stop. Though his legs were weak, Fauja's spirit was strong.

As Fauja got bigger, it was time to go to school. But the school was miles away from his small village. There were no buses. Fauja's legs could not carry him all that distance, and they couldn't bring the school to him.

So while Fauja's friends went to school, he got his education on the farm, learning to plant, plow, and pick all kinds of crops.

"It's too hard. He's too weak," said the neighbors.

But Fauja did not listen
and Fauja did not stop.

He'd walk behind the buffaloes, planting seeds and getting stronger with each step.

Fauja worked and worked and worked. He walked and walked and walked. He farmed and farmed and farmed.

And when Fauja turned fifteen, the whole village witnessed a new wonder:

Fauja could walk an entire mile!

Fauja progressed by leaps and bounds, and he took many big steps over the next few years.

He got married, he had children, and he even got his own farm.

Fauja loved life in Punjab. He loved flying kites in the open fields with his children. He loved the excitement of a close cricket match played with friends. And he loved the joy that filled the village during the harvest festival of Vaisakhi.

He taught his children how to farm, just like his father had taught him.

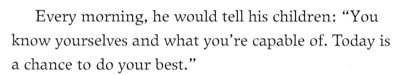

Every morning, he would tell his children: "You know yourselves and what you're capable of. Today is a chance to do your best."

He cherished every step in his life's journey.

As time passed, Fauja's children grew up and moved to places far away. Fauja, who was usually lively and energetic, grew sad and lonely, especially after his wife died.

He missed his family and wanted to be with them.

But to leave his village at the age of 81 to go live on the other side of the world! Could Fauja do it?

His friends were worried. "You're too old, Fauja," they said. "It's too hard for you to move away."

But Fauja didn't listen and Fauja didn't stop. He knew it was time for him to take a step in a new direction.

One day, Fauja got on an airplane for the first time and went to live with his family in England.

It was cold in England, and almost everyone only spoke English. Fauja was used to having many friends, but here he felt like a stranger.

His family was busy with school and work. Fauja found himself with nowhere to go and nothing to do.

Fauja passed his days in the living room, staring at the television. He had never been so miserable.

As he was flipping channels one day, he saw something new. A whole lot of people were running around town.

Was it a fire? An accident? No, Fauja realized. They were running just to run! And they all had big smiles on their faces.

Fauja knew at once that he had to try this.
He put on his shoes, then walked out the door.
He took one step. And another. Then another, and another, and another . . .
Fauja Singh was running!
The wind flowed through his beard,

and for the first time in a long while,
a smile appeared on his face.

After that day, there was no stopping Fauja. He began by running a little bit every morning.

As he got stronger, he ran faster and longer, and when he felt especially strong, he would even run again in the evenings before eating daal and roti with his family!

In England, it was common to see people running for fun, but not many of them looked like Fauja Singh. Some people would stare and some would laugh, but Fauja did not let that bother him. He ran and ran through the streets and parks of England, getting better and better each day.

He ran races, and he ran for fun. He ran with his friends, and he ran alone, always with a smile on his face. Fauja loved running. He liked the new friends he made. He enjoyed exploring the new country he now called home. And he loved how being outdoors reminded him of his childhood, of playing hopscotch and flying kites in the fields. It had been a long time since he felt this happy.

More than anything, Fauja loved the challenge. He had always enjoyed pushing his limits, whether it was learning to walk, doing farmwork, or moving to a new country. Now he was ready for his next challenge. He started training with a coach, Harmander Singh, who had run many marathons and had trained others to run marathons too.

There was no looking back after that!

Harmander and Fauja ran together many times a week. After months of hard work, 89-year-old Fauja Singh became one of the oldest people to ever complete the 26.2-mile London Marathon!

FINISH

FLORA
1999

FLORA
2000

Fauja ran the London Marathon five more times after that,
getting faster each year and setting new records each time.

By this point, Fauja was famous. As people in England followed this man with a beard, turban, and disarming smile running great distances, they began to learn more about his Sikh background.

Around this time, Fauja learned that some people in the United States were attacking Sikhs for how they looked. Fauja knew this was wrong and he wanted to help, but he wasn't sure how to share his message.

He couldn't read. He couldn't write. He couldn't speak English.

But he could run . . . and at once, Fauja knew what he had to do.

He decided to run the world's biggest
marathon in New York City!
    By now, Fauja was 93 years old.
Could he still run 26.2 miles?
    Many news reporters didn't think so.

he's too weak
it's too
hard

But Fauja did not listen and Fauja did not stop.
Every day, he practiced with his coach.
Every night, he dreamed about running.
And every morning, he reminded himself of his mother's words:
"You know yourself, Fauja, and you know what you're capable of.
Today is a chance to do your best."

The big race finally came on a chilly November day in 2003. Fauja Singh stood at the start line. He felt ready, knowing he had prepared as well as he could. He stretched in anticipation and recited a prayer, envisioning what it would feel like to cross the finish line.

Just then, someone shouted racist and hateful words at him. Other people joined in.

Fauja brushed it off. He knew he had a strong spirit.

He ran, one foot in front of the other . . . and then disaster.

The tender blisters on the soles of his feet had burst, and he was in a world of pain. He kept going, limping to the finish line. He made it, but it was his slowest time ever.

Fauja was so exhausted that he collapsed right after the race. Medics wanted to rush him into an ambulance and take him away to recover, but Fauja preferred to stay and recover in the company of his trainer and fellow runners.

Fauja made it back to England, and for the first time in a long while, he was sad. Fauja had wanted to run fast and show the world what Sikhs could achieve. But he felt like his poor performance at the world's biggest marathon made him look weak and that he had failed his Sikh sisters and brothers all over the world.

FAUJA'S FALL

"*Maybe they were right,*" said a voice in his mind. "*Maybe it is too hard. Maybe you are too weak.*" The voice made Fauja doubt himself for the first time in years, and it tried to convince him to quit running altogether.

But Fauja did not listen. Inspired by his coach, he set a new goal for himself.

He was going to be the first 100-year-old person to ever run a full marathon!

Fauja ran every single day for years. He ran and ran. He practiced and practiced. He trained and trained. And when the day came, he knew he was ready.

On October 16, 2011, 100-year-old Fauja Singh lined up at the start for the Toronto Waterfront Marathon. He was so excited that it felt like an electric current was flowing through his body.

He ran along the course, and people joined him for a few miles at a time to show their support. He welcomed them with a smile, offering jokes to adults and high fives to children.

As he ran, Fauja thought about all the things people had said he would never do.

They said he couldn't walk . . . but he did.

They said he couldn't farm . . . but he did.

They thought he was too old to run . . . and yet, here he was, running 26.2 miles at the age of 100.

Fauja had never been more sure of himself. He hoped that children and adults everywhere would see him take on this difficult challenge and persevere with grace—something he'd learned through his faith.

It took him just over eight hours*, but he finally did it. Fauja Singh finished the Toronto Marathon and set a new world record as the oldest person to ever run a marathon.

He stood tall and smiled proudly, holding tightly to his medal. He had faced many challenges in his 100 years,

but Fauja Singh always kept going!

*Fauja's final time was 8 hours, 11 minutes, 5.9 seconds

MORE ON FAUJA SINGH

Fauja Singh is a Sikh, a Punjabi word meaning "student." Although he is now one of the oldest people in the world, he is still constantly learning. The religion he practices, Sikhism, is the world's fifth largest. It originated in Punjab nearly 500 years ago, the same region where Fauja Singh was born and lived for most of his life.

As part of his faith, Fauja Singh never cuts his hair and always wears a turban. Sikhs believe in treating everyone equally, serving others, working hard, and living with honesty and integrity. Fauja Singh has been practicing these values for more than 100 years now. Being a Sikh has been a core part of Fauja Singh's identity since his childhood, and he believes firmly that his successes in life are tied to what he has learned from his Sikh faith.

Fauja Singh met his coach, Harmander Singh, when he was 88 years old. Harmander is an accomplished runner who has completed over 160 marathons and is an official pacer at the London Marathon and the Toronto Waterfront Marathon. After Fauja Singh decided he wanted to run the London Marathon, he worked with his coach every single day for more than a decade. His coach ran with him and cared for him, and the two of them became trusted friends. They remain very close to this day.

Jeff J Mitchell / Getty Images

FAUJA SINGH'S RECORDS

National Records (United Kingdom)

Fauja Singh holds many national records for runners 90 years of age or older. These were set at Mile End Park Stadium in East London on July 2, 2005:

- 200 meters – 45.13 seconds
- 400 meters – 1 minute, 49.28 seconds
- 800 meters – 4 minutes, 20.97 seconds
- 1 mile – 9 minutes, 40.13 seconds
- 3,000 meters – 18 minutes, 38.48 seconds
- Marathon – 5 hours, 40 minutes
  (Set on September 28, 2003 in Toronto)

World Records

Fauja Singh has set several world records for runners 100 years of age or older. These were set at the Ontario Masters Athletics Fauja Singh Invitational Meet on October 13, 2011:

- 100 meters – 23.40 seconds
- 200 meters – 52.23 seconds
- 400 meters – 2 minutes, 13.48 seconds
- 800 meters – 5 minutes, 32.18 seconds
- 1,500 meters – 11 minutes, 27.81 seconds
- 1 mile – 11 minutes, 53.45 seconds
- 3,000 meters – 24 minutes, 52.47 seconds
- 5,000 meters – 49 minutes, 57.39 seconds
- Marathon – 7 hours, 49 minutes, 21 seconds
  (Set on April 22, 2012 at the London Marathon)

While many running organizations have recognized his records, the Guinness Book of World Records has yet to officially honor Fauja Singh as the world's oldest marathoner. Guinness does not accept Fauja Singh's government documents and requires a birth certificate—even though India did not begin registering births until 1969, 58 years after Fauja Singh's birth. Fauja Singh and the UK government recognize the year of his birth as 1911.

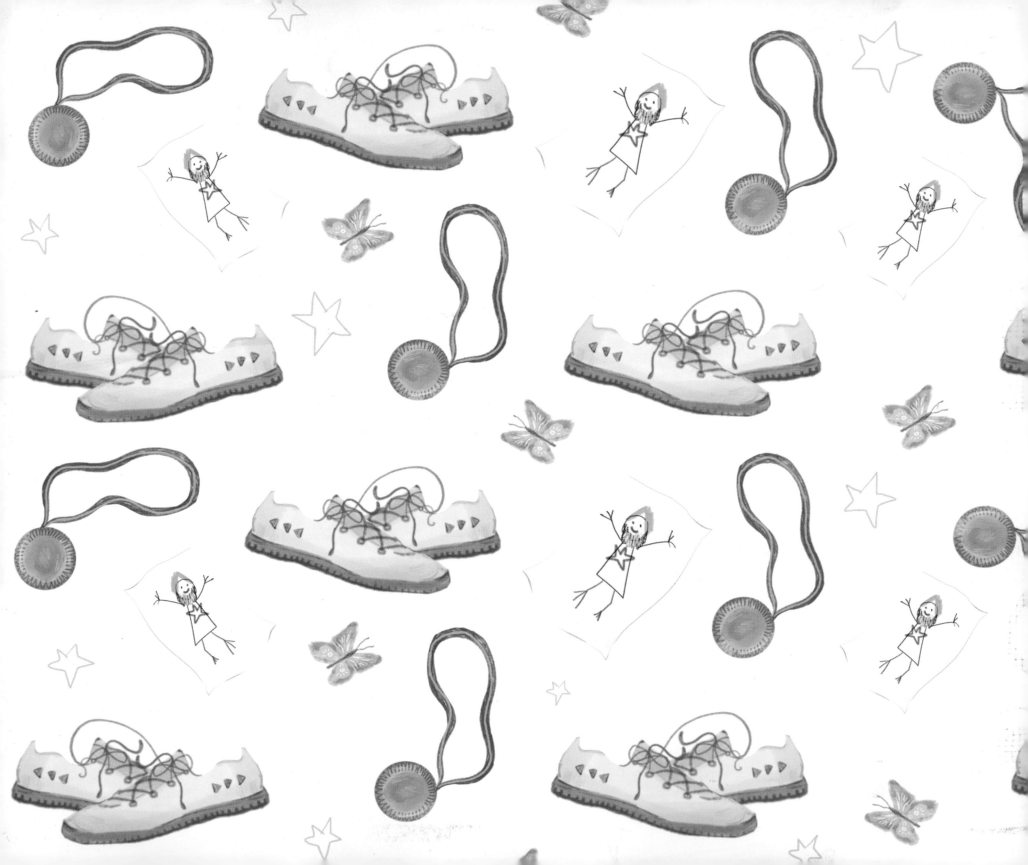